The World of
FLOWER
ARRANGING

The World of
FLOWER
ARRANGING

Barbara Pearce

NEW YORK

Photographic acknowledgments
Ken Lauder: front cover, pages 21, 23, 35, 40, 43, 48, 50, 54, 59, 61.
Michael Plomer: back cover, endpapers, frontispiece, pages 6, 7 top, 7
bottom, 8, 9 top, 9 bottom left, 9 bottom right, 10, 11, 12, 13, 14, 15, 16,
17, 18 top, 18 centre, 18 bottom, 19, 20, 24, 25, 26 left, 26 right, 27,
28 top, 28 bottom left, 28 bottom right, 29, 31, 32 top left, 32 top right,
32 bottom, 33 left, 33 right, 36 left, 36 right, 37 top, 37 bottom, 39, 41,
42 top left, 42 top right, 42 bottom, 44 top, 44 bottom, 45, 46, 47, 49
top, 49 bottom, 51, 52 left, 52 right, 53, 55, 56 top, 56 bottom, 57, 62,
63, 64.

Line illustrations by Ian Garrard

Contents

Practicalities of Arranging

Longer Lasting Flowers

I hope that by the time you have read this book, you will have gained enough basic know-how and confidence to become a successful flower arranger. For simple reference I have divided the book into two parts. The first section deals with the preparation and choice of flowers and containers together with descriptions of the mechanics available, i.e. the tools and aids used to hold the plant material in the arrangement. In the second part I have explained how to do eight basic arrangements, detailing the guide lines you need to know in order to create attractive arrangements for yourself and many different examples of how you can adapt the basic arrangements to suit favourite containers, flowers and room settings.

Before attempting to arrange a collection of flowers and foliage, however, it is most important to spend some time on giving the plant material the necessary treatment so that it will last longer in the finished arrangement. All flowers and foliage will benefit if they are given a long deep drink in a bucket which has been almost filled with tepid water. First, however, the ends of the stems should be treated so that they will take up water more readily. This preparation is necessary because, after flowers have been cut, the sap at the end of each stem dries quickly and forms a seal. The following treatments should be carried out both when the flowers are given their initial drink and also, if you need to cut them again, when they are finally arranged. Remember to put them into water immediately after they have been prepared.

Soft stems, for example tulips, can usually take up water easily. Cut each stem on the slant – never straight across as there is then a danger that it will rest on the bottom of the bucket and will be unable to take up sufficient water. This cannot happen when the stem is cut at an angle as it then rests on the tip of the point. Such a cut will also give a larger area through which the stem can drink.

Hard and woody stems, for example carnations and chrysanthemums, have greater difficulty in absorbing water.

It is better to cut a soft stemmed flower at an angle as shown on the tulip on the right, not straight across as on the left.

Make a slit up the centre of the end of each stem for about 1 inch (25 mm). Alternatively, hammer the end of each woody stem so that the tissues are crushed. I find that hammering woody stems is quicker when preparing them for the initial drink, but when cutting them to the required length for an arrangement, it is more convenient to slit them.

When hollow stems, like those of the lupin, are placed in water their tip ends always turn upwards which tends to spoil the final arrangement. To prevent this turn each flower upside down over the sink and with a small watering-can fill the stem with water. Do this very carefully to avoid air bubbles forming. Then you can either plug the stem with a small piece of florists' foam (Oasis) or cotton wool and place it in the bucket of tepid water or simply hold your thumb over the bottom of the stem, put it into the water and take your thumb away. The pressure of the water in the bucket will keep the stem filled with water.

Above: Hard stemmed flowers need to be cut up the centre of the stem from the bottom as shown with this carnation.

Left: The alternative way to treat a hard or woody stemmed flower, e.g. chrysanthemum, to enable it to take up water more easily, is by hammering the end of the stem.

Hot water treatment for a wilting rose is to place the bottom of the stem in an inch (25 mm) of boiling water, protecting the head with tissue paper.

When you cut the stem to the required length for the arrangement do this under water. If you need to cut a treated stem when it is out of water turn it upside down. You can then cut it to the required length without losing any water.

Dahlias and young spring foliage will benefit from hot water treatment and it is also possible to revive flowers which droop after they have been in an arrangement for a day or two by dipping their ends into boiling water. This is particularly so with greenhouse-grown roses. Bring a pan of water to the boil and place the bottom inch (25 mm) of the stems into the water, having first protected the flower heads from the steam by wrapping them in either tissue paper or polythene bags. Leave them in the water for about twenty seconds and then take them out and place in tepid water which comes nearly up to their heads.

When some stems are cut, they give off a white milky substance and they are said to be 'bleeding'. Examples of flowers

with this type of stem are members of the euphorbia family and poppies. Holding the ends of such stems in a match or gas flame for a few seconds will stop the bleeding. Again the petals should be protected.

All the hellebores including Christmas and Lenten roses, cyclamen flowers and polyanthus will last very much longer if their stems are slit up for about 1 inch (25 mm) on one side, starting an inch from the bottom.

Certain flowers and foliage – young spring foliage, artichoke leaves, violets and hydrangeas amongst them – last better if they are completely submerged while being given their initial drink. Violets take in a great deal of water through their petals and, even after submerging them for the first drink, it is advantageous to spray them overhead occasionally in the arrangement. If hydrangeas wilt after they have been arranged, they can be revived by placing the flower heads in water. They will take

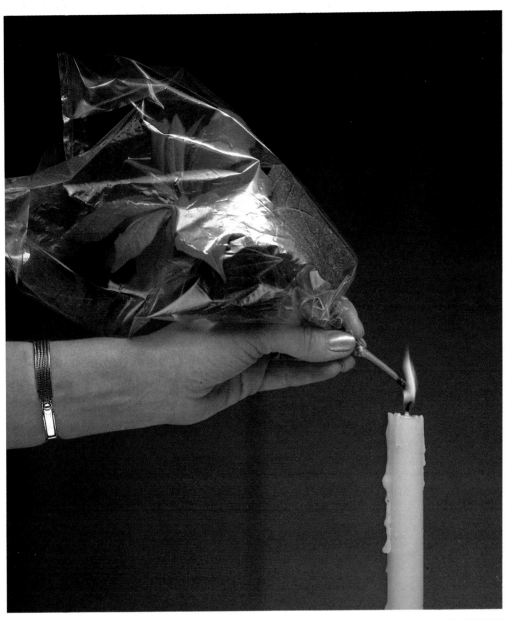

Left: Burning the end of a stem that 'bleeds' over a flame. The head of *Euphorbia pulcherrima* (poinsettia) is protected by a polythene bag.

Far left: The side of a stem of *Helleborus niger* (Christmas rose) is slit with a knife about an inch (25 mm) up from the bottom of the stem for about 1 inch.

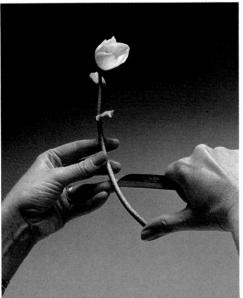

Left: Submerging a leaf which is soft for its initial drink.

9

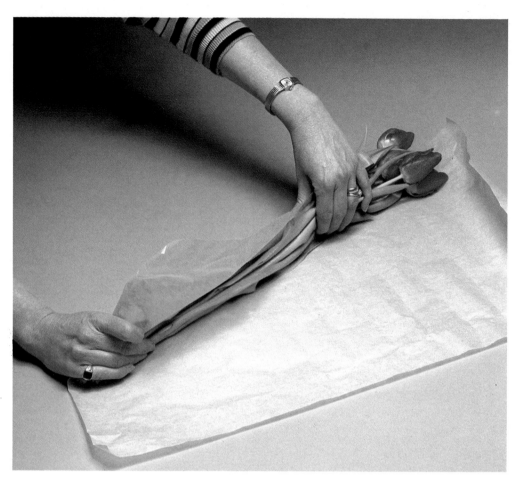

Placing a bunch of tulips on greaseproof paper, prior to rolling them. Rolling tightly helps to keep the stems straight.

in water through their bracts and will quickly become refreshed.

And now for some general hints on the care of flowers and foliage. It is best to use warm water for the initial drink as flowers seem to accept this more readily and are refreshed quicker than when cold water is used. It is also important that flowers are not left out of water for too long as they wilt very quickly. The anemone is particularly vulnerable.

Sometimes it is necessary to keep flowers for a time before they are arranged. If this is the case first treat them, put them in a bucket for their initial drink and then place this in a cool place, preferably on a stone floor. Roses can be rolled tightly in greaseproof paper to stop them opening too quickly.

Tulips, as I am sure most people have found out, are not the easiest flowers to arrange because their stems curve towards the light. The stems can be straightened by rolling them tightly in greaseproof paper and then placing them in deep water. Unfortunately, after a day in an arrangement, they will tend to revert to their old ways.

The water level in the container holding the arrangement should be looked at each day. On the first day it is advisable to look at it night and morning but afterwards once a day should be sufficient provided the room is not excessively hot. When topping up use tepid water as the water in the container can become fairly warm and it is rather a shock to the flowers if they are suddenly given cold water.

Before flowers and foliage are arranged, the leaves which will be submerged should be removed. If these leaves are left on, the water will quickly smell unpleasant but with clean stems it should stay comparatively fresh. It is not usually necessary to change the water once the flowers have been arranged but if clean water is needed, it should be tepid.

Some leaves and flowers have 'hairy' stems, for example *Begonia rex*, which can act as a syphon draining water out of the container to leave a pool of water on the furniture. To avoid this remove the hairs from that part of the stem which goes beneath the water by scraping it.

The bunch of tulips rolled in the greaseproof paper, before being placed in a bucket of deep water.

Branches of lichen also need to have the ends of their stems cleaned for the same reason.

The Right Container and Accessory

The choice of containers and accessories is very important as they can either make or completely spoil an arrangement. Points to look out for are the suitability of the flowers and foliage to the container, the shape of the container in relation to the proposed shape of the arrangement, and the position of the finished arrangement in a room. First I shall describe the different shaped containers in detail and explain how and where each can be used.

CONTAINERS

Tazza I find this elegant container the most useful of all. It is wide but shallow and is mounted on a stem which always gives an air of grace. The wider the top of the container the easier it is for arranging flowers and this is one of the reasons why I would always recommend a beginner to buy a tazza first.

It is very versatile, lending itself to many arrangements either for the centre of a table or for facing arrangements (symmetrical or asymmetrical) against a wall.

Bowls Although not as elegant as the tazza, bowls are extremely useful. They look well in low all-round arrangements for the centre of a table. When used like this they are often known as posy bowls. They will also successfully accommodate facing arrangements (symmetrical or asymmetrical).

Large bowls are used in pedestal arrangements. A mixing bowl, painted in a colour to match the pedestal, will do admirably. It is surprising how often kitchen bowls will double up for flower arranging to save the expense of buying a special container.

Urns These are great favourites with flower arrangers. They are tall and usually fairly thin and as such are very graceful. They are more difficult to arrange because of their limited width and extra care needs to be taken when using them, as will be demonstrated later in the book. They are only suitable for facing arrangements (symmetrical or assymmetrical). All-round arrangements never look right in them because of the urn's relative height and width. This shape of vase looks attractive in a niche.

Oval This shape, either as a flat oval dish or mounted on a stem, is probably most useful for a table centre and it looks especially lovely on an oval table. It will also hold facing arrangements (symmetrical, asymmetrical or L shaped) for a mantelpiece or similar position. When a symmetrical arrangement is created in an oval dish, it is better to keep it longer and lower than for a similar arrangement in either a tazza or urn.

Cylinder This is a very popular shape as it looks well in modern homes. It is not the easiest shape to arrange because of the narrow opening at the top, but when the right plant material is used it can be most attractive. It is usually unsuitable for a traditional setting in a room furnished with antiques. However, in certain circumstances the two can be blended together. An arrangement in a cylinder needs to be very tall and thin in keeping with the shape of the container.

Troughs These are long and low and can be used as table centres. They are particularly good for long tables at formal dinners, or on mantelpieces, window-sills and shelves. They make excellent containers for church window-sills. A facing arrangement (symmetrical, asymmetrical or L shaped) in a trough can either be long and low or it can be quite tall, depending on the position in which it is placed. Wide troughs are particularly suitable for line arrange-

A selection of flower containers. To the rear an urn, left a dolphin, right a narrow-necked vase and in the foreground a basket with handle.

ments. Troughs are made of various materials such as china, copper, brass, silver, pottery, wrought iron and basketwork.

Baskets These can be found in a variety of shapes and when they are made out of basketwork they are especially suited to country-type flowers and informal arrangements. China and glass baskets are also available and these can contain more formal arrangements. Those fashioned out of basketwork will require water-tight linings and baking tins can be used successfully. These will need to be painted in order to seal them so use a colour to match the basketwork. It is best to have a matt finish paint as this is less conspicuous than a gloss. This inside container must be level with the rim of the basket so may need padding beneath.

Baskets with handles are extremely popular and there is a great range available both in size and shape, including the trug basket. This is more difficult to use than most because of the low handle which needs to be seen after the flowers have been arranged.

Very pretty arrangements can be created in baskets with lids but these containers are not quite so useful as those with handles as they are unsuitable for all-round arrangements. Never cover all the lid with flowers and foliage.

Shells Containers fashioned in the shape of a shell are pretty for flower arrangements. Try, however, to keep the shape of the shell which usually results in a long, low arrangement.

Adaptable containers Some containers can be used which were not originally

A more contemporary selection of containers. At the back a heavy pottery vase, to the right a bamboo cylinder, at the front on the left a shallow pottery bowl and to the right an oval pottery trough.

13

An arrangement of mauve and purple anemones with santolina, *Senecio greyii* and large ivy leaves in a shell. Note the arrangement is kept relatively low in keeping with the shape of the container; otherwise it is arranged and the flowers and foliage grouped as for a facing arrangement.

meant to hold flowers. Many Victorian *objets d'art* can be converted. Needlework, writing and Bible boxes have great potential and can become favourites for flower arrangements. They will need water-holding linings and painted baking tins are again ideal. The lids of such boxes make good backgrounds to the flowers and they can be very attractively lined with material. Pieces of wood cut to fit inside the lid can be covered with different coloured and textured materials attached by transparent sticky tape. In this way a range can be built up so that you will have the appropriate colour and also texture of material to go with whatever flowers and foliage you want to use. Make sure that the material looks right with the particular wood of the box. For shiny woods satin or velvet look well.

Only facing arrangements can be done in these boxes and an L shape is ideal.

Victorian oil lamps can also be used from time to time by making a simple conversion. Remove the wick and replace it with a candle-cup. Glass oil lamps look beautiful with matching flowers but lamps can also be found in china, silver and gilt. Arrangements can be all round or facing but if the lamp is very tall it will look better with a facing arrangement.

Silver meat covers make splendid flower containers if they are inverted on a stand. You may be able to find someone to make a wrought-iron stand for you and if you are going to make a lot of use of such a container have two stands made – a low one for table centres and a taller stand for facing arrangements (symmetrical or asymmetrical).

Vegetable dishes and frying pans make original containers. Brass frying pans are particularly good especially when arranged with red or orange flowers. With a little imagination a wealth of containers will be found in the kitchen. A meat plate with a small water-holding container made out of an empty salmon tin would make an excellent container for a line arrangement.

Dual-purpose containers   I have already mentioned the various types of containers such as the tazza which can be used for more than one type of arrangement. If you do not want to buy many containers or if you have limited storage space, the following are the best: tazza, bowl, trough and basket with a handle.

ACCESSORIES

Flower scissors   Specially designed flower scissors are available and are essential equipment for the arranger. They incorporate two useful features – a serrated edge which is useful for cutting heavy stems and a wire-cutting groove.

Candlecups   These are small containers which are designed to fit on to candlesticks. They are available in various sizes and they can also be fitted into the necks of bottles which make appropriate flower containers for parties. Candlecups are made in chrome, brass, copper, and white or coloured plastic and are inexpensive. Although they can be used for facing arrangements, they are better suited to all-round ones. If you have a three-branched candelabra around which you would like to create an arrangement, either fit a candle-cup on each side and leave the centre free, or have one candlecup in the centre and leave the two sides free. When using a candlecup for an all-round arrangement, a candle can be included in the centre.

Cones or tubes   Although these are seldom needed for arrangements in the home, they are excellent when creating pedestal arrangements in churches or for receptions. They are used to give extra length to stems when it is impossible to obtain flowers with long enough stems to

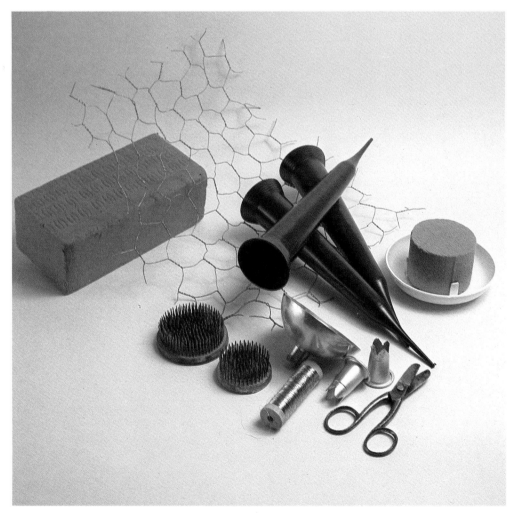

A selection of equipment used at various times by the flower arranger. Included are florists' foam, wire netting, tubes, pinholders, candlecup, candle holders, silver reel wire and scissors.

15

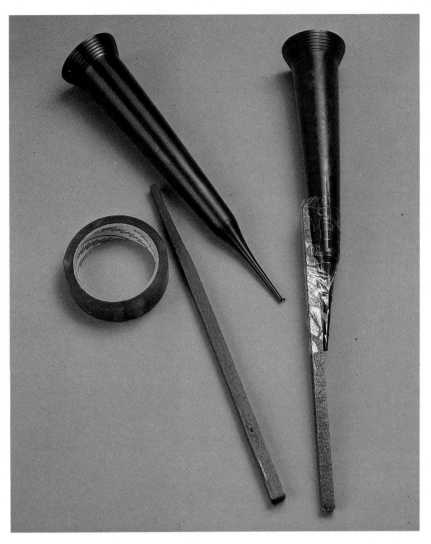

A tube or cone being attached to a green square stick with transparent sticky tape. Some flowers would be placed in the cone when doing a large arrangement to give extra length to stems.

achieve the correct proportions in large arrangements.

First attach the cone to a green-painted square stick with transparent sticky tape so that cone and stick overlap by about 3 inches (75 mm). A square stick is better than a round one because a round one will tend to twist in the netting, whereas a square one will hold its position. The length of the stick depends on the height of the arrangement and the length of the flower stems. For a pedestal arrangement three cones are usually sufficient but in a really vast arrangement as many as twenty could be used. This, however, is exceptional.

Blocks of glass These are useful to place at the base of the container in a line arrangement to cover the pinholder. Position them so that they run through beneath the flowers and foliage. The glass will look like ice and give an illusion of coolness and so it is particularly lovely in summer arrangements. Colourless

glass is more natural than coloured, but coloured glass can be used to match up with a particular flower. Take care, however, as some flowers like the chrysanthemum never look very happy with glass arranged beneath them. If you are unable to obtain small pieces of glass they can be made by using glass from shattered windscreens which you may be able to get at your local garage. Cover a pebble with silver paper. Paste this over with a strong clear glue and then completely cover the pebble with two layers of the shattered glass. Shattered glass may also be used on its own.

Pebbles These can be used in a similar way to glass. I have collected many different ones from river banks and the seashore. Their colours can be beautiful – white, pink, grey, brown and mauve. Some have metallic streaks in them and it is usually possible to find a pebble which echoes the colour of a particular flower. They are preferable to glass in the more unsophisticated or country type of arrangement which uses daffodils, dahlias and others. They are also more at home in the heavier pottery containers.

Both pebbles and glass should be placed so that they present a casual appearance. They do, however, need careful positioning so that they enhance the design of an arrangement and do not spoil the effect.

Shells These can be used in arrangements of seashore flowers such as sea holly (eryngium). Coral also makes an interesting accessory.

Driftwood This is very much sought after by the flower arranger and it can be very difficult to find a piece with a really good shape. Although driftwood can be bought, often it has been bleached and I prefer it in the natural state – you will certainly value it more if you are lucky enough to find a piece for yourself. Beaches and the shores of lakes are the more likely hunting grounds. If it is the right shape, driftwood can form part of the actual container for the flowers but generally it is used as an accessory and is particularly effective in simple arrangements using just a few varieties or, better still, one kind of flower.

Figurines These are mainly used as accessories in competitive flower arranging in helping to interpret a theme like a song or book title. They should be less

important than the flowers and foliage.

Candles These make effective and useful accessories, especially when creating an arrangement in a candlecup. They are also attractive in the centre of long and low arrangements where they can give height. A candle holder is placed in the centre of such an arrangement to hold the candle. This has spikes in its base to attach to florists' foam or a pinholder.

How to Hold Flowers in Their Containers

In this chapter I shall describe the various methods used to hold plant material in position in an arrangement. Everyone has their favourite aid and as each new one comes on to the market, it is tried and tested and usually the flower arranger finds that it has a particular part to play. I must admit, however, that I still prefer the old method of wire netting for the majority of arrangements.

Wire netting I use a mesh of 2 inches (50 mm) and to me this is preferable to the smaller size which is available. It can be rolled tighter if needed for thinner stems and there is more space to take larger stems without damaging them.

You will find by means of trial and error how much netting is required for a container. This varies with the type of flower to be used and the thickness of the stems. On the whole the stems of spring flowers are thicker than those produced during the rest of the year so less netting will therefore be needed for these.

Useful accessories for the flower arranger. A piece of driftwood, pebbles, shells and coral can all be used on different occasions to add interest to an arrangement.

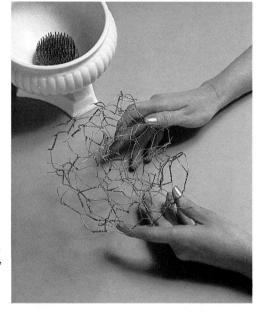

Three stages of putting wire netting into a container. In this instance the container is round with a pinholder in the centre. First roll the netting diagonally from one corner to the other – this makes four or five layers of netting. Secondly, shape to the container. Thirdly, place it in the container and secure by clipping small pieces of netting over the edge.

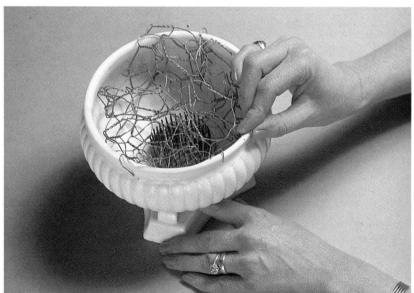

The wire netting must be firmly secured in the container otherwise you are unlikely to achieve a successful arrangement. First select the size of netting required, then consider the depth and width of the container. It is impossible to give exact measurements of the piece of netting needed for a certain container as some people like a little more and others less. As a rough guide, however, a medium-sized bowl needs about 18 to 27 inches (45 to 70 mm) of 18-inch (45-mm) high, 2-inch (50-mm) mesh. It is much better to have one large piece of netting. If you only have two smaller pieces then it is advisable to join them together by twisting the edge of one around the other.

Next loosely roll the netting from one corner to the other so that you end up with four or five layers. After it has been rolled in this way consider the shape of the container to be used. With a bowl or tazza, the two ends need to be bent right into the centre and the netting gently forced into a rounded shape. With an urn, keep the netting narrow at the bottom then push it into the container. When a trough is being used bend the ends of the netting in a little way. Some of the netting should touch the bottom of the container and it should be level with the rim and slightly raised in the centre where the longer stems are placed. Spread the netting evenly out in the container.

The next step is to secure the netting and this can be done in two ways. If the container has a lip, some of the edges of the netting can be clipped over this. Five or six strands fastened at equal distances are sufficient to hold the netting firmly and they will be hidden once the arrangement is completed. If there is no suitable lip then the netting will have to be tied into the container. Thirty-gauge silver wire, which can be purchased on a reel and is similar to fuse wire, is the best for this purpose. If silver wire is not available then a fairly fine string can be substituted. Tie the wire or string around the container as if you were tying up a parcel and finish by knotting firmly at the top of the netting. If the container has a stem then take the wire around this once or twice and then tie it both ways over the bowl. If, after the arrangement is completed, the wire or string is noticeable, it can be cut away and the flowers should remain in position. If you are using a china container then the netting could be secured with transparent sticky tape. However, never do this with valuable containers as it can mark them. This is especially so with silver, copper, brass, pewter and other metalware.

It is not necessary to remove the netting each time an arrangement is dismantled. Rinse the container thoroughly under the tap before putting it away and occasionally take out the netting and give the vase a good scrub.

Water-retaining substances There are several types of florists' foam on the market (probably the best known in Britain is Oasis). This needs to be thoroughly soaked so that when the stems of the flowers are anchored into it, they do not meet any dry patches.

Florists' foam can be cut to the required shape whether it is wet or dry. It can be used on its own in a goblet-type or any small container but when it is used in a larger vase with bigger flowers then a small piece of netting placed over the foam and tied into position is an advantage. Unfortunately, florists' foam is more costly than wire netting because it cannot be used indefinitely. After it has been used for three or four arrangements it crumbles and will not grip the stems.

Never fill a container completely with florists' foam as it will then be difficult to give the arrangement more water. This needs to be done as the flowers drink water from the foam at the same rate as a conventional arrangement using wire netting and the water level should be checked regularly in the same way.

Florists' foam is difficult to use with soft-stemmed flowers but stiff-stemmed flowers will be anchored quite firmly. With daffodils or similar-stemmed flowers, you may have to make a hole in the foam first with a pencil and then put the flower stem into this.

Holders for florists' foam These are useful when the foam is used on its own. Although similar to a pinholder (see later), they only have about six spikes which are each about $1\frac{1}{4}$ inches (32 mm) high. The foam is placed on to these spikes and is held firmly by them. They are useful when using heavier branches because the extra weight at the base helps to balance the branch.

Cradles for florists' foam These can be made when glass containers are being used. Although it is quite in order to see the stems of the flowers through the glass, you should not be able to see the mechanics. Take a small piece of wire netting and push the centre about 2 inches (50 mm) down inside the container and clip the edges around the rim. When this netting is firmly in position, put in the soaked foam so that it comes just above the rim of the glass container. Three-quarters fill this with water. The stems of the flowers and foliage are then pushed into the foam. The tallest ones at the back can go straight down into the container. The flowers which come out over the edge should be placed horizontally into the foam. Make sure that the leaves and flowers over the edge cover the foam cradle as this should not be seen when the arrangement is completed.

A glass vase with a cradle of wire netting to hold florists' foam. The outer edge of the netting is clipped over the vase to secure into position.

Pinholders These are one of the most useful aids to flower arrangement and they are available in different sizes. They are used underneath wire netting in shallow containers to hold the heavier stems at the back of an arrangement. This can save much time and patience as it will prevent the longer-stemmed flowers moving. Florists' foam can be used in a similar way.

Another use for the pinholder is in a line arrangement on a flat dish. A heavy pinholder is needed, preferably one which is lead based so that it holds the flowers without toppling. It may be necessary to stick the pinholder to the container with Bostik Blu-tack or a similar re-usable adhesive, but I would advise against this if at all possible as some adhesives may spoil the surface of the container. If the flowers are balanced correctly there is no likelihood of their falling over. It is certainly worth paying extra for a heavier pinholder. You can buy pinholders with the spikes close together or further apart. For heavier-stemmed flowers and foliage you will need the spikes further apart.

A candlecup placed onto a narrow necked vase can be attached with silver reel wire or a reusable adhesive such as Bostik Blu-tack round the edge to hold it in position. The candlecup gives more space to arrange flowers and enable flowers to come horizontally over the edge of the container more easily.

Gravel Sometimes when large heavy flowers are used in a container which is relatively light, the arrangement can become unstable and topple. This should not happen if the finished arrangement is correctly balanced but you might run into difficulties when making it up. Gravel or even sand can be placed in the bottom of the container to make it heavier. The gravel will not harm the flowers and will not take up too much room in the container.

Pedestals When using flat, relatively light bowls on pedestals, these should be attached to their stands with string or thick wire to hold them firmly in position. When the container is heavier and urn shaped this is not necessary. With a pedestal arrangement in a marquee, it is advisable to anchor it well as the ground is more uneven and it could topple. If a wrought-iron pedestal is to be used, this can be staked to the ground.

Narrow-necked containers These include the narrow-necked altar vases which are found in many churches. They are extremely difficult to arrange because there is only room for perhaps two or three stems in their necks. To overcome this secure a candlecup in the neck with silver wire. Alternatively a funnel, which has been plugged with a cork to stop the water running through, can be used in the same way.

Colour Schemes in Flower Arrangement

Colour plays a very large part in successful flower arranging. If an arrangement has a good colour balance but is lacking in other respects it will still be attractive and receive attention. The appreciation of colour is a very personal thing and I am purposely not going to be over technical. Here, however, are some colour schemes and ideas to help you.

Monochromatic This is a colour scheme which uses the tints and shades of one particular colour or hue and it can be very attractive. The tint is the hue with white added and the shade the hue with black added. Extreme care should be taken to make sure that the colours are correct. For example with pink flowers you will need to use either the blue pinks or the yellow pinks as mixing the two will not give the blending of

colours necessary for this scheme. You will soon acquire a flair for this, however, although it is not always easy to obtain just the colour of flower which you may require to do this kind of arrangement. It is impossible for a florist to carry a full range of all the colours.

Clashing colours This scheme uses the clashing colours contained inside one hue and it can be great fun. For a red arrangement you will need the blue reds and also the yellow reds, going from magenta to a bright orange. It is surprising how attractive this can look, especially on a dinner table where it will provide a good talking point. Red probably lends itself better to this colour scheme than any other hue but pink can also be used successfully in this way.

Analogous To explain an analogous colour scheme you really need to picture in your mind a colour wheel. First think of the colours of the rainbow – red, orange, yellow, green, blue, indigo, violet – and then form them into a wheel by putting the red next to the violet. To take this a step further, imagine this central circle flanked by an outer circle of the same colours with white added giving the tints and an inner circle with black added to give the shades. In this way an arrangement can be built up on a red, red-orange and orange scheme or a yellow-green, green and blue-green theme and so on. This is a very useful type of colour scheme especially when it is impossible to obtain shades and tints of one colour. When using this type of scheme try to use the lightest of the colours at the top of the arrangement and also on the widest points as they will show up so much better.

An arrangement using the tints and shades of yellow. The flowers are arranged in a converted writing box with a baking tin lining. The arrangement is L shaped so part of the lid can be seen. The flowers used are stock, broom, tulips, roses, hyacinth, polyanthus and Cheerfulness narcissi, with limey green coloured foliage. Make the arrangement as the basic L shape.

Mixed colours Many people like to see mixed colours in an arrangement and this can be achieved in one of four different ways. The first is known as a Dutch group and this borrows the colours from a Dutch flower painting. The second way is with mixed garden flowers. The third uses the Victorian idea of colour and the fourth pastel shades.

The Dutch flower paintings are remarkable for their colourful arrangements of flowers from different seasons. Tulips, often striped ones, fritillaries, pheasant eye narcissi, poppies, open roses and many others are seen together. It is fun to study the colours and types of flowers in these paintings although it is not necessary to copy them exactly but simply to follow along the same lines and to make your arrangements as mixed as possible.

For an arrangement of garden flowers go into the garden and collect one or two of each kind and colour of flower. It is best to leave out the white flowers because the eye immediately goes to these and is detracted from the rest. If you do use white place it near the centre of the arrangement. Lime-green flowers are very good in a mixed arrangement. They blend in well and lend a sharpness to the composition. There is a surprisingly wide selection of green flowers such as *Alchemilla mollis, Amaranthus viridis,* lime-green nicotiana, the green zinnia called Envy and many of the euphorbias. Yellow flowers bring out the colours of others, so try to include them. It is better to choose different shaped flowers which will give added interest.

The Victorian idea of colour was rather hard and they used bright and gaudy hues. Try to use the flowers which would have been available then such as geraniums and pack them in tightly or place them in an epergne or a piece of Victorian glass to complete the effect. These Victorian arrangements will, of course, look especially attractive in rooms furnished with antiques.

Pastel colours are especially effective when used in small spring arrangements of flowers such as pale pink roman hyacinths, primroses, blue muscari, pale green hellebores and mauve freesia. They are also useful for a children's party decoration and one pretty idea which should delight a small girl is to lead trails of ribbon from an arrangement to each child's place at the table with a present on the end. Pastel-coloured flowers look well when arranged in a natural way by having clumps of flowers on a dish with bun moss. The dark green of the moss sets off the pastel shades.

Complementary These are the colours which are opposite to each other in the colour wheel and an arrangement using them is most successful when they are of equal intensity, for example clear red with clear green or apricot with cobalt blue.

Arrangements of one colour with white Pastel colours are nicer to use with white because they do not provide such a contrast. Red and white are better not seen together for this reason, apart from the fact that many people are superstitious about using these particular colours.

Foliage colour With any colour scheme of flowers, it is usually possible to obtain foliage which complements it. For example red flowers blend well with reddish foliage or red-stemmed foliage; pink and blue flowers look well with grey foliage; orange flowers with leaves tinted and shaded orange. Yellow flowers are especially good with yellow and lime-green foliage, and white flowers also look attractive with lime-green leaves. The foliage belonging to the flowers being arranged is always suitable and it is, of course, more natural, but if the foliage colour does match the flowers it adds that extra something.

Coloured containers These can cause problems because of matching the flowers to them. The most useful colour is dull yellow-green as many different coloured flowers will look well against it. White containers can be rather obvious and create too great a contrast to the colour of the flowers. Orange and other brightly coloured containers are useful for some colours but can be limiting.

Silver and pewter containers are particularly good arranged with whites, pinks, mauves and, especially at Christmas time, reds. Copper is ideal for red and orange flowers and for mixed green flowers and foliage. Brass is excellent with yellow flowers and again a mixed green colouring. Basketwork is better with orange, red, mixed colouring and yellow.

The colour scheme of the setting An arrangement should not look too obvious in a room. It should blend in with the furnishings and become part of the surroundings. This does not mean that you need to use the same colour scheme and flowers every time. When a room is designed around two colours you can emphasize one of these colours one week and the other the next. The third week the two colours could be blended together. You need not use the exact colour of the room but a tint or shade of the colour. This will again give interest. You can also vary the containers so that the shape of the arrangement will change too. Use mixed flowers of the chosen colour or just one kind of flower and change the position of the arrangement in the room.

If a room has been furnished in neutral colours then an arrangement to brighten it will be attractive. A Dutch group could be used in this case. If there is a painting on the wall, compose an arrangement using flowers in the same colouring. A mirror is a useful feature because by creating an arrangement of mixed greens to reflect into it, an impression of coolness can be achieved and this can be effective especially in hot weather.

When sending a gift of flowers try to remember the colouring of the room they will be going in. If this is not known keep to neutral colours like cream.

It is important to take into account the light intensity of the room. Blue, for example, is a very poor colour if the room is fairly dark, especially if it is being

Above: The use of green gives an impression of coolness in hot weather. The broom gives height and the heather and Boston fern (*Nephrolepis*) are grouped one way and asparagus fern and periwinkle (*Vinca*) the other. In the centre are scindapsis leaves, parlour palm (*Chamaedorea elegans*) and *Helleborus foetidus*. The arrangement is the same as a basic facing arrangement.

Opposite page: As the vase is decorated I decided to have a simple line arrangement with five red chrysanthemum blooms and *Mahonia bealei* leaves. In the top of the container is wedged a piece of florists' foam.

used with lighter coloured flowers such as white. In any case never use blue at the top of an arrangement with white flowers immediately beneath. The blue flowers will disappear leaving the white standing out well and this will make the arrangement an odd shape. Any colour which has blue in it will not show up well in a dark room and this includes the blue pinks, blue reds and purples. Yellow flowers and colours with yellow in them will show up very well from a distance, whereas the blues will not. Keep blue for daylight rather than artificial light.

Special occasion flowers and their colours Good flowers will make an occasion even more special. Send golden-yellow flowers for a golden wedding anniversary; use pink flowers for a girl's christening. These colours may be very traditional but I think people still prefer to keep to them. For a girl's twenty-first

or eighteenth birthday link the colours of the flowers with the colouring in her dress. For a wedding I think the church flowers and also those for the reception should echo the dresses of either the bride or the bridesmaids. In the church the white or cream of the bride's dress are best as these will show up well in the darkness of the church.

If you regularly arrange flowers for the church, you will know that certain festivals need special flowers and colours.

Choosing Your Plant Material

The choice of flowers and foliage to be used is of the utmost importance in flower arranging especially as the interest is partly derived from this aspect.

Flower types For the purposes of arranging, flowers can be classed into three groups. First there are the pointed

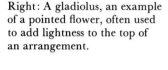

Right: A gladiolus, an example of a pointed flower, often used to add lightness to the top of an arrangement.

Far right: A spray chrysanthemum gives a bunchy appearance as the flowers come from secondary stems. They can look a little heavy as the tallest flower in an arrangement unless they are pruned slightly.

26

flowers. These have many flowers borne closely on each stem. The pointed effect is produced because the flowers gradually open in succession starting with the lowest. Those at the top are only in bud form when the flowers at the bottom are at their best and so the spike gradually tapers to a point. Examples include gladioli, delphiniums, larkspur and stocks.

The second group also have many flowers to each stem but each of them is borne on a separate secondary stalk to give a bunchy appearance. Examples include spray chrysanthemums with flowers originating from all down the stem and alstroemerias with the flowers deriving from one point at the top of the stem.

The third class comprises the flowers which are carried singly at the end of one main stem. These flowers have a variety of shapes. There are both single and double kinds, those with flat faces and those with trumpets. Examples include daffodils and many members of the daisy family.

When creating an arrangement of mixed flowers, it is better to combine these various shapes. Pointed flowers will make good main outline flowers to an arrangement as they will provide an air of lightness. Do not use bunchy flowers high on the periphery of an arrangement unless you are able to use even larger material lower in the outline as this will look top heavy and you will ruin the effect. Ideally it is better to use two kinds of pointed flower.

The value of grouping will, I hope, become clear to you when you start to do some of the basic arrangements. Grouping gives a more even distribution of weight and therefore good balance. Smaller flowers should always be used on the outline edge and higher throughout an arrangement with the larger flowers nearer the centre and lower.

If you combine single and bunchy flowers in an arrangement, you will find that you will need more single flowers to balance the multi-headed ones. When using only single flowers try to get as much variation of shape as possible.

Foliage types The choice of foliage needs the same consideration. Single leaves have various shapes. They can be broad and rounded like the bergenia;

oval and pointed like hosta; heart shaped like the leaf of the arum lily; irregular like *Begonia rex* or have a serrated edge like the artichoke. These leaves are used to give heart to an arrangement especially when light spiky flowers are incorporated. Their weight will help to hold an arrangement together and to give it solidity. Even when doing a small arrangement you can still use larger leaves in the centre though, of course, these should be in scale with the rest of the plant material. Ideal in these circumstances are ivy and scindapsis. An uneven number of leaves are used in the centre but it would be very unusual to need more than nine. These leaves should not be overcrowded as this would defeat the object of keeping a clean cut centre. You can also use whole rosettes of leaves in the centre of an arrangement instead of large, single leaves. House plants, aspidistras and

Flowers on a single stem have a variety of shapes. They can be single or double: an example is the daffodil.

27

Right: There are many different shapes of single leaves for flower arranging. An extremely useful one is the bergenia.

Below: A compound leaf for flower arrangement is the *Senecio greyii*. This type of foliage has a multiple leaved stem.

Below right: Tall thin leaves are usually placed upright as they normally grow this way: an example is the sansevieria.

caladiums for example, can be a very attractive source of such material.

For our purposes compound leaves can be described as those with many leaves to a stem and these can be grouped with the flowers through an arrangement. It is better to have two kinds of this type of foliage in an arrangement so that one kind can be arranged with one group and the other with the second. Examples include pittosporum and senecio with the individual leaves quite small and Portuguese laurel and gaultheria which are quite large. When choosing the foliage to go with certain flowers try to get a good contrast to provide interest and balance. If the flowers are fussy, select a clean cut foliage like gaultheria. If, however, the flowers are single, a more fussy foliage like pittosporum could be used.

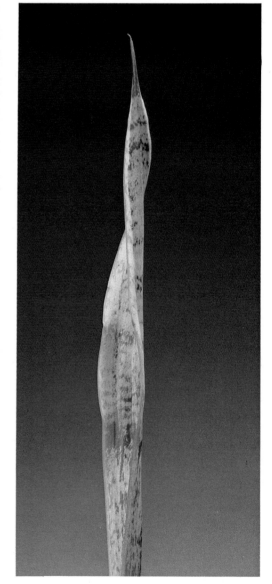

Twigs and branches are very good for flower arrangement. In this heavy pottery container there are the twigs of *Viburnum fragrans* which form the outline with some through the centre. The three chrysanthemum blooms are near the centre with bergenia leaves.

Lastly, there are the tall thin leaves. Since these grow naturally upright, they should be positioned reasonably vertically in an arrangement. This type of leaf is valuable for establishing the height of an arrangement. Do not make a fan of them as this looks particularly ugly. Examples are Sansevieria and reeds.

Ferns These can be used upright in an arrangement or sideways along the edge as both ways will emulate their natural habit.

Grasses These will add lightness and interest to an arrangement. Many seedsmen offer a wide variety of ornamental grasses from which you can make a selection if you want to try growing some of the many different forms in your own garden. As with tall thin leaves arrange grasses upright.

Twigs and branches These are very useful for giving shape to a line arrangement and for providing interest in a mass arrangement.

Lichen-covered branches are found in damp areas. The lichen is formed by the symbiotic association of a fungus and an alga i.e. a fungus and an alga existing together for their common good. It is often found on fir trees but if you can find it on less brittle wood then these pieces can be stored for several years without disintegrating. When arranging lichen-covered branches that portion which is to go under water should be scraped free of lichen as this will syphon water out of the container.

Alder trees are generally found beside rivers, ponds, lakes and other damp habitats and the twigs are attractive in winter and spring with their small cones and catkins. The catkins do not produce their pollen until the spring but they are still excellent for winter decoration.

The bracts of the lime tree develop in high summer though these might not be readily noticed when the tree is in full leaf. If you are lucky enough to have access to a tree you can judiciously cut off some of the elegant stems. Trim away the leaves to reveal the lime-green bracts. You could use the stripped lime so prepared in both mass and line arrangements.

Stripped lime can be preserved with glycerine and it can then be kept for several months. To do this slit the ends of the stems and give them a short drink. Then place the bottoms of the stems into a solution of one part glycerine to two parts hot water. Leave them for a week to ten days until the lime has turned an attractive brown colour.

Hazelnut catkins are firm favourites with flower arrangers and most attractive when used with daffodils. Other catkin-bearing subjects include the willow and one species has the additional interest of contorted branches. Pleasing arrangements can be achieved with just a few catkin branches and a group of large leaves beneath to cover the pinholder. The pretty branches of daphne are beautiful in association with just a few flowers which pick up the colour of the daphne. *Hamamelis mollis* is another good early-flowering shrub, as is *Chimonanthus fragrans* and *Viburnum fragrans*.

Many other beautiful woody subjects can be found in garden and countryside. It is important, however, when you are cutting twigs from a shrub or tree that you do this very carefully so that you do not spoil its overall shape.

Bulrushes These give the flower arranger another interesting shape. They should be used upright and several of differing lengths placed at the top of an arrangement working down towards the centre will prove very attractive. I think that the natural-coloured ones are to be preferred to the dyed ones.

Berries and seedheads These are invaluable for arrangements from September to November. They can be used on their own with just a little foliage or combined with both flowers and foliage. There are many attractive berries available in a wide range of colours. It is, therefore, quite easy to match a particular flower with a berry. Heavier sprays of berries are best kept to the centre of an arrangement but lighter branches can be grouped throughout. If necessary, clip some of the leaves off the branches to show the berries more clearly but do not completely defoliate them.

When using seedheads with just a small amount of foliage, try to have as many different shapes as possible. Examples include clematis, both cultivated and wild, delphiniums, lupins, poppies, honesty, philadelphus, buddleia and teasels.

Availability of plant material You may not be able to find some of the flowers which I have used in the arrangements in this book and I hope that this will not deter you for there are many other similar flowers which can be substituted. Some of you will not have a garden but a wealth of material can be gathered from the hedgerows and many of the flowers can be bought from the florist. If you only have a small garden and would like to cultivate some material for arranging, I would strongly recommend you to grow foliage rather than flowers. It is far easier to buy flowers than foliage – at least, interesting foliage. You can even grow a few ivies, which are most useful for flower arrangement, in a window-box.

How many flowers? It is very difficult for a beginner to determine how many flowers are needed for a mass arrangement. This depends on the size of the container, where the arrangement is to be placed and the size of the flowers. It is not easy for me to give you much guidance in this respect but as an example a medium-sized urn with a facing arrangement would need roughly 40 flowers. The right judgment will come with experience and when you become accustomed to your containers. You will then be able to tell by eye the number of flowers you will need when picking from the garden or buying from a florist.

Never overcrowd an arrangement; each flower needs space around it. It is always better to have too few rather than too many flowers. Remember, too, that a bud will open into a flower and always leave sufficient space so that when it does open it will not smother its neighbours.

The amount of foliage used is fairly critical. A massed arrangement with fewer flowers will need more foliage. When using leaves as fillers to the flowers do not put in too many as a forest effect can quickly be achieved. Foliage will look most untidy unless it is used with care.

If you are to have less than a dozen flowers in an arrangement keep to an uneven number. The tendency is to arrange an even number in pairs which will result in a very regimented effect. With an uneven number this is unlikely. Also have an uneven number of leaves.

Flowers with their own foliage It will look more natural if the foliage of the flowers to be arranged can also be used, in which case it must be grouped through the arrangement with the flower to which it belongs. Leave the compound leaves of roses attached to a piece of the main stem. This will help when securing them into an arrangement. Tulip leaves are sometimes rather large and heavy. To overcome this, they can be cut short and the cut ends rolled round pieces of stem which will help to hold them into the netting. Daffodil leaves are very attractive when used with their flowers.

A line arrangement with nine roses with their own foliage in a black pottery dish. The roses are placed on a pinholder. Because of the simplicity of the arrangement some pebbles have been placed in the dish to add interest.

Choosing flowers suitable to the container is quite important. In the arrangement shown in three stages the daffodils, being a country type of flower, look well in a basket. This round handled basket has a cake tin lining. The first stage is the seven points around the edge, and the tallest ones in the centre. The second stage is more flowers between the outline ones on the edge and the variegated privet put throughout. The third stage is building flowers and foliage from the outline to the tallest flowers as for the basic all-round arrangement. Some leaves of the daffodils can be placed in threes of various lengths.

Opposite page, left: A pedestal arrangement in a mixing bowl painted black with a block of florists' foam under the netting. There are three tubes which are established first quite close together three-quarters of the way back in the container. The outline flowers are placed in, with the grouping as for a basic facing arrangement.

Bunches of three or five are more effective especially if each leaf in the bunch is placed at a different length. They should not be longer than the flowers.

Dahlia foliage is good but it should receive hot water treatment before being arranged. Peonies, too, have long lasting leaves. These should be cut leaving a piece of main stem attached as for roses. These are just a few examples of leaves which can be used with their own flowers.

The right flower for the container
Another aspect to consider is the suitability of flowers to the container.

Daffodils, a country-type flower, do not look right arranged in a sophisticated glass container. They look their best in basketwork, brass, copper, heavy-type pottery and cork bark. Roses can be arranged in a variety of containers. Florists' roses look quite well in glass or porcelain. The more robust-looking garden roses of yellow, orange and red shades look very happy in basketwork. Arum lilies are most attractive arranged with their own foliage on a flat glass or china dish so that the water can be seen around them. Chrysanthemums are quite adaptable to containers and they look well in basketwork, copper, brass, pottery and silver. A mixture of summer flowers is lovely in a basket. In fact all garden-type flowers are attractive in basketwork containers. The more sophisticated flowers look well in silver, glass and porcelain.

Here is a suggested list of what colour and texture of container would most readily suit a particular flower. *Red flowers* – copper; wooden boxes; black pottery; basketwork; pewter. *Orange flowers* – copper; stone; basketwork; gilt. *White flowers* – white china; silver; gilt; mirror; plain, blue or green glass. *Pink flowers* – silver: pewter; plain, pink or green glass; green, white, grey or pink china. *Blue flowers* – grey, green or white china; silver; plain, blue or green glass; mirror. *Yellow flowers* – green or white china; brass; wooden boxes; basketwork; gilt. *Green flowers* – green pottery; brass; mirror; glass. *Mauve flowers* – grey or white china; silver; pewter; mirror; glass. With a combination of colours choose a container suitable for all of them.

Large arrangements The flowers and leaves for large arrangements need to be on a much bigger scale than arrangements for the home. Big bold flowers will always look more effective as these arrangements are usually seen from a distance. It is still necessary to incorporate the different shapes of flowers and foliage and there are a host of large flowers and leaves which could be used.

Flowers to suit the style of the setting
Try to use flowers which blend in with the room setting. For example an ultra-modern room needs modern line arrangements with just a few flowers to match the colour of the room. A Victorian room should have an arrangement in a Victorian container. The elegant room should have an arrangement in a tazza or urn and for a country cottage a basket of mixed garden flowers is the most attractive.

Below: The completed pedestal arrangement. The grouping of the flowers and foliage are nine lilac, eleven carnations and skimmia foliage going high on the left to low on the right. Nine guelder rose (*Viburnum opulus*), eleven iris and rhododendron foliage go the opposite way. The centre flowers and leaves are three stems of Longiflorum lilies and three bergenia leaves.

Eight Basic Arrangements

Introduction

This section includes detailed descriptions of eight basic arrangements explained in an instructional manner. To avoid repeating myself I have assumed that for each arrangement you will choose and prepare your plant material and container as advised in the first section of this book.

You will not have the exact containers as those shown in the photographs but as long as they are of a similar shape and care is taken in selecting the flowers and foliage to go in them you will be successful. I am sure that if you use different materials when creating the arrangements which follow you will find it more challenging and far more rewarding when they are a success.

I have summarized below the main principles which should be applied when creating successful arrangements as a rough guide to help you remember and these points are explained more fully in the arrangements which follow.

1 Grouping is perhaps the most important factor in obtaining a balanced effect. Remember when choosing your flowers to select a good variation in shape, together with an attractive colour balance.

2 Good variation of stem length throughout an arrangement is also necessary. Never have two flowers of the same length side by side.

3 Keep the larger flowers lower in the arrangement and the smaller ones of each kind on the outline and throughout the arrangement to give a light touch.

4 All the stems should appear to radiate from the tallest in the arrangement.

5 Never have crossing stems in an arrangement.

6 Always position a stem so that the flower head is exactly where it is required. Never try to move a flower head after the stem has been secured.

7 Leave plenty of space around each subject in an arrangement especially buds which will open and expand. Do not overcrowd the flowers.

8 Try to keep the arrangement as natural as possible. This depends to a large extent on the shape and curvature of the stems to be used. The flowers should never be rigid and they will look more natural if some of them are placed so that they are facing to the side rather than looking straight ahead, especially if they are flowers with an 'eye', i.e. a single flower with a flat face.

9 When using mixed flowers, it is better to have at least three different kinds of flower but two would be permissible.

10 A broken line around the edge of an arrangement is very important. This is created by having the flowers in the outline at different lengths so that they give an uneven impression and not a trimmed look.

11 Never make the main flowers in the centre of an arrangement look too obvious. Other plant material, which is lighter in weight and longer stemmed, should be arranged through the centre.

12 When creating a facing arrangement always remember to fill in at the back to hide the netting and give a finished appearance.

13 Arrangements should never look flat when they are seen from the side. By building out from the tallest flower at the back to the longest over the front edge with lighter weight flowers you should be able to achieve a triangular effect from this angle too. The line drawings show-

Opposite page, right: The line drawings show various stages of the basic facing arrangement. The flowers used are campanula (A), larkspur (B), carnation (C), rose (D) and peony (E). The campanula and carnation form one group, the larkspur and roses another going the opposite way. The centre flowers are in pink with the large leaves, hosta (F), in green. The first stage is the outline points. The second stage is the placing of more flowers in the outline and the flowers and leaves in the centre. The third stage is the overall shape and shows the grouping of the filling material, escallonia (G) and *Senecio greyii* (H), while the fourth stage is the side view showing how it is built from the top flowers to the bottom outline edge flowers.

Opposite page, left: The completed basic facing arrangement in a tazza using campanula, larkspur, carnations, roses and peony with escallonia, *Senecio greyii* and hosta leaves.

ing the arrangement viewed from the side are designed to help you avoid falling into this trap.

14 Plant material known as filler is used to cover the mechanics which should not be seen when the arrangement is finished.

15 The size and shape of the container should always be considered when choosing the plant material and the style of the arrangement. The container and the finished arrangement should appear as one complete unit and not two separate parts.

16 If any of the plant material is top heavy, some of the side shoots can be carefully cut away and the prunings so removed used lower down in the arrangement when filling in. Make sure, however, that the cuts are not noticeable in the finished arrangement.

17 Whenever possible try to arrange flowers where they will finally be viewed. It is then much easier to take into consideration their setting.

18 Fill the container three-quarters full of water before beginning the arrangement, and after the flowers and foliage are arranged fill to the top of the container.

Facing Arrangement in a Tazza

The symmetrical facing arrangement can be created in a variety of containers but I shall explain in detail how to do it in a tazza as this is one of the easiest for a beginner to use. Place a medium-sized pinholder in the tazza about three-quarters of the way back in the centre, then fit in the wire netting as explained in the first section. I have chosen five different kinds of flowers in two colours to show the groupings more clearly. The pointed flowers are a bunch each of pink larkspur and white campanula and the round ones are five white carnations and seven pink roses. Three pink peonies have been selected to give weight in the

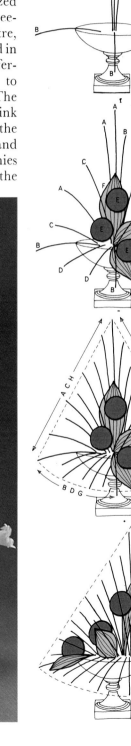

35

Above: The start of a facing
arrangement in a green bowl
in reds showing the outline
flowers. These are three
gladioli, two spray chrysanthemums and a carnation.
Note how the flowers are
brought from high on one side
to low on the opposite side.

Above right: In the next stage
more flowers are added around
the edge and the three chrysanthemum blooms with the
bergenia leaves in the centre.
Note the grouping as for the
basic flower arrangement. The
gladioli, carnations and snow-
berry and skimmia foliage are
one way, and the cotoneaster
berries and holly foliage
with the spray chrysanthemum
the other way.

centre of the arrangement. I have
grouped the white flowers together to
follow one direction through the arrangement and the pink flowers will go the
opposite way. For the foliage, I have
selected escallonia to go with the pink
flowers and senecio with the white and I
also have three large hosta leaves for the
centre.

When you have prepared the flowers
and the container and are ready to begin,
select a campanula with a comparatively
small flower. This will be the tallest stem
and its height should be at least one-and-
a-half times the height of the container
and preferably twice. Secure this flower
three-quarters of the way back in the
centre of the container. All the facing
arrangements which I shall describe, be
they symmetrical, asymmetrical or L
shaped, start three-quarters of the way
back in the container. This is because if
the arrangement were to start at the back
of the container, the flowers which would
be necessary to fill the space and come
well out over the front edge would
appear to bulge in the centre and the
shape would be lost.

After you have positioned this first
flower, take a second campanula with a
slightly larger flower but a shorter stem
and place this a little to the left side of
the first campanula so that it is secured
through the same hole of the netting and
is adjacent to the first stem on the pin-

holder. Next take a small larkspur, cut it
a little shorter than the second campanula and place it to the other side
(right) of the first campanula, again
securing it through the same hole of
netting.

Establish the widest points on each side
of the arrangement so that the overall
width is roughly the same as the height.
It is important to choose flowers which
have curved stems so that they arch over
the edge and join the arrangement with
the tazza. In this way the flowers and the
container appear as one unit and not
two separate parts. Place a campanula
on the opposite side to the second
campanula, thus following the line of the
grouping through, and a larkspur on the
other side. Both these stems should be
three-quarters of the way back in the
tazza and of equal length. They should
be as horizontal as possible but be well
into the water.

All the stems in this arrangement, as
indeed in any other, should appear to
radiate from the tallest. However, they
should not all touch it and some,
especially those which form the outline,
should only go half way towards it. If all
the stems were to extend back to the
tallest, this would lead to such a tre-
mendous confusion and crossing of stems
that a successful arrangement would be
impossible to achieve.

When you have positioned the stems

Left: The finished arrangement in red flowers completed as for the basic facing arrangement, each group of flowers connecting through the centre. Leycesteria berries are also placed near the centre.

Below: For guidance to see how flowers build out from the top flowers to the front outline edge, a side view of the arrangement.

demarcating the width, place a small pointed flower – I have used a larkspur – over the centre front edge of the tazza in line with the tallest campanula at the back. This becomes the longest flower at the front of the arrangement and completes the positioning of the main outline flowers. None of the subsequent stems should exceed these in length or the shape of the arrangement will be lost.

Proceed by joining up these principal outline flowers around the edge, remembering to keep your flowers in their groups. In this case the white flowers extend from high on the left to low on the right with the pink larkspur and roses arranged in the opposite direction. Bring the stem lengths down quite quickly at the back to achieve a triangular rather than a fan shape and make a good semi-circle around the front. Aim for a broken line around the edge with plenty of variation in stem length to prevent the arrangement from becoming too set.

Now that the outline is completed, place in some of the foliage. Keep the escallonia and rose foliage with the larkspur and roses and the senecio with the white flowers and follow the line of the flowers through, placing some foliage fairly high and some low to cover the netting. You will find that it is easier to fill in with foliage and cover the netting as you are doing the arrangement rather than leaving this important part until you have nearly finished.

The peonies and hosta leaves are used to give a heart to the arrangement and are positioned next. The large centre flowers should not be kept in a straight line but should be arranged in zig-zag fashion. Only three large centre flowers are being used for this particular arrangement but often five or even seven are incorporated. The important thing is to get a good balance. Although an arrangement needs weight in the centre, the effect should not be too heavy. The large leaves are positioned to frame the main flowers and an uneven number is again used to prevent the arrangement from appearing too regimented.

Place the largest peony low into the centre with a smaller one above the first and a little to the right. The third peony goes low over the right front edge. The leaves should be positioned so that one goes over the right front edge, one goes at the back facing the one at the front and the largest leaf goes low into the centre and turned slightly sideways.

It is essential that the groups of flowers should be connected through the centre so that they merge together, and here are a few words of advice which will apply to all arrangements. Good variation of stem length is important. Never have two flowers of the same length side by side. The smaller flowers should have the longer stems and be positioned high through the arrangement whereas the stems of the larger flowers should be cut so that they can be placed lower into the arrangement. Be careful not to make the arrangement look flat when it is viewed from the side. Even from this angle it should still present a triangular appearance. Position some of the flowers so that their heads are facing sideways as this creates a more natural effect. None of the flower stems should cross one another and they should all appear to radiate from the base of the tallest.

When all the flowers are in position, check that the netting is covered, especially at the back, so that if the arrangement is seen from the side it will not present an unfinished appearance. The netting should be covered with short pieces of foliage. Some longer pieces can be used to cover the stems of the flowers and disguise the stalky effect

which might develop. Do not overdo the foliage, however, as this might ruin the whole arrangement.

Study the arrangement by standing away from it and make any necessary adjustments.

All-round Arrangement

In my description of the method for doing this type of arrangement, I have used a silver dolphin container but you could do exactly the same arrangement in a flat bowl. A small pinholder is needed for the centre of the container over which the wire netting should be secured. There are five garnette roses of the variety Carol, fifteen grape hyacinth (*Muscari*), eleven freesia in pink and mauve, seven pieces of pussy willow and five pink ranunculus. The pointed subjects in an all-round arrangement, like the pussy willow in this one, should be generally short, otherwise they will give the finished arrangement a spiky appearance.

The foliage for this arrangement is small so that it does not overpower the flowers or the container and I have chosen trails of leaves from pot plants – zebrina, variegated ivy in a grey tone and five leaves of saxifrage in a grey-green colour so that all the foliage is of a mauve or grey colouring. Also included are a few rose leaves to place in low with the rose group.

For an all-round arrangement, I find it easier to establish the shape around the edge of the container first. This is done by having an uneven number of outline points. In this arrangement I have seven but a smaller arrangement would only need five whereas a large one would take nine or even eleven. The more outline points used the easier it is to get a good shape. For the outline flowers I have chosen one rose, two freesia, one grape hyacinth, two pussy willow and one ranunculus.

It is preferable to introduce each kind of flower into the outline though this is not possible when a particularly short-stemmed variety of flower is being used. The outline flowers chosen should be the smaller ones of each variety as this keeps the arrangement lighter around the edge. All the outline stems are exactly the same length from the edge of the con-

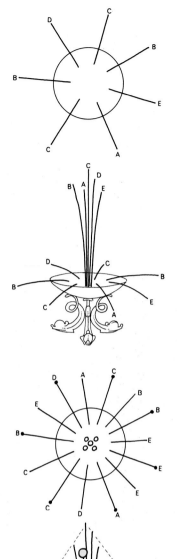

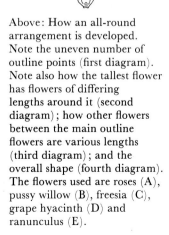

Above: How an all-round
arrangement is developed.
Note the uneven number of
outline points (first diagram).
Note also how the tallest flower
has flowers of differing
lengths around it (second
diagram); how other flowers
between the main outline
flowers are various lengths
(third diagram); and the
overall shape (fourth diagram).
The flowers used are roses (A),
pussy willow (B), freesia (C),
grape hyacinth (D) and
ranunculus (E).

tainer to the top of the flower in order to
ensure that the round shape is kept. They
should also be placed roughly the same
distance apart. If two of each kind of
flowers are being used to create the outline then they should be on opposite sides
of the arrangement. However, if fewer
varieties of flowers are being used, three
of one kind may be needed on the outline.
In this case place one flower on one side
and two adjacent diagonally opposite.
Should the outline contain four of a
kind, place two adjacent on one side of
arrangement and the other two diagonally opposite to these. The flower stems
go horizontally into the container about
half way into the centre. They are, of
course, below the water line. The flowers
should extend well over the edge of the
container but not so far as to overpower
it. For the size of this dolphin container,
which is approximately 4 inches (100
mm) in diameter, about 2 inches (50 mm)
over the edge is sufficient. The size of the
arrangement is obviously related to the
amount of plant material available but
always allow the flowers to overlap the

container. Never stop at the rim as this
will give a stuffed appearance and the
arrangement will not flow well. All the
flowers in an all-round arrangement
should be aimed towards the centre.

When the main outline flowers have
been placed in position, the height can
be determined. In a small arrangement
like this the height can be the same as the
overall width. The flower chosen to
establish the height needs to be small and
if possible pointed. I have chosen a stem
of freesia which is pink and will show
up better than a blue or mauve flower.
The height can vary according to where
the finished arrangement is to be placed.
For a table arrangement it needs to be
kept low so that it does not block the view
of anyone.

When the tallest flower has been
placed in position and firmly established
on the pinholder, place a few flowers of
various kinds around and close to it.
None of them should be as tall and each
one needs to be a slightly different
length. Usually four flowers around this
centre one are sufficient to create a pretty

pointed top to the arrangement. The width and the height of the arrangement will now have been established and none of the subsequent flowers or leaves must go beyond these points or the shape will be lost.

Now go back to the outline flowers around the edge of the container and place flowers of varying lengths between them. They need to be practically as long as the main outline flowers but do not place all of them to exactly the same length as you will then achieve the effect of a circle within a circle. A less set pattern is required. Conversely if these flowers are cut too short and placed in against the rim of the bowl, a star-shaped arrangement will be made and not a round one. It is very important when you

are creating an all-round arrangement to keep turning the container round all the time. The danger is that you will complete one side and not have enough flowers left over to do the other. You may also end up with a very uneven effect.

The grouping of the flowers should run from one side to the diagonally opposite side, i.e. roses opposite roses, grape hyacinth opposite grape hyacinth, pussy willow opposite pussy willow. When looking down on to the top of the arrangement, however, the flowers should not be seen in a straight line across the bowl. There should be a slight zig-zag effect across to the opposite side. One flower group can merge with the flower group beside it e.g. a grape hyacinth can merge with the roses so that the flowers do not

Opposite page, right: The basic all-round arrangement using small flowers in a small silver dolphin container. The flowers are in pink, blue and mauve and include small roses, grape hyacinth, ranunculus, freesia and pussy willow. Grey-coloured foliage goes with them.

This arrangement in a candle-cup on a candlestick is an adaptation from the basic all-round arrangement. The general principles are the same but it is kept lower in the centre as the candle gives the height. The arrangement is mainly foliage but heathers and *Helleborus foetidus* have been added as they are green in colour. Keep each kind of foliage going from one side to the opposite side.

This is an all-round arrangement in a white pottery bowl shown in stages of development. The method of arranging is as for a basic all-round arrangement. The flowers on the outline in the first stage are two yellow single spray chrysanthemums, two yellow spray carnations, two double cream spray chrysanthemums and one apricot double spray chrysanthemum. The tallest flower in the centre is a small spray carnation with an introduction of the other kinds of flowers around it. In the second stage three orange gerbera have been used near the centre with bergenia leaves. More flowers are placed around the outline with foliage in the arrangement, each kind being grouped through and including ivies (*Hedera*) and variegated privet. The final picture is the completed arrangement.

look too set like slices of cake. The foliage should be grouped with the flowers and some used to cover the netting. I have rose leaves with the roses, zebrina with the ranunculus and grape hyacinth, small saxifrage and ivy leaves with the freesia and ivy leaves with the pussy willow. In this way the foliage and flowers in each group complement one another. The zebrina foliage is fairly solid against the light grape hyacinth. The ivy looks well with the pussy willow and some of it can be used to trail over the edge of the container.

Connect up the flower groups in the arrangement, placing the larger heads lower down. Do not place any of the same kind of flower in a straight line and merge the groups well together. Keep turning the arrangement around all the

42

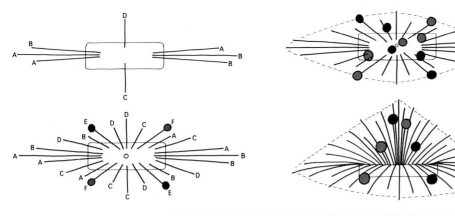

Top left: Line drawings to show various stages when arranging a basic table centre. The grouping goes diagonally across the arrangement, and the flowers used are mont-bretia (A), hypericum (B), single spray chrysanthemum (C), double spray chrysan-themum (D) and two kinds of dahlia (E and F). The main outline is achieved as in the first diagram, showing the length and width. The other flowers on the outline are placed within these main out-line points, and the tallest ones in the centre (second diagram). Foliage goes through and also the larger flowers in the centre, these being the two kinds of dahlias. The first three line drawings show a plan view of the arrangement, the last how the flowers and foliage are built up from the outline to the tallest flower.

Left: The basic table centre uses apricot and orange coloured flowers, kept long and low, arranged in an ovenware dish.

time and fill in with foliage where there is netting showing. Do not overcrowd the flowers as each should be clearly seen.

Table Centre in a Trough

There are many trough-like containers available and even an oblong glass dish from the kitchen would be suitable. The container which I have selected is a rectangular shallow oven-ware dish. I have placed a small square of florists' foam in the centre of the dish under the wire netting but a pinholder would serve equally well.

I have chosen apricot and orange shades to achieve an autumnal effect. Pointed flowers are scarce when chrysanthemums and dahlias are easily avail-able, and, as gladioli would be far too heavy for this table centre, I have selected fifteen montbretia. If you are unable to get pointed flowers then autumn berries are an excellent substi-tute. In fact, I have also chosen nine stems of hypericum berries to balance the montbretia and there are three berried sprays of viburnum and three of berberis. The round flowers consist of two stems of single and three stems of double chrysanthemum sprays with five each of two kinds of dahlia. The indi-vidual flowers from the sprays of chry-santhemums can be used singly.

The seedheads of physalis – Chinese lanterns – are particular favourites of flower arrangers and I have three sprays. I have removed the leaves from the stems as they are rather overpowering and tend to hide the lanterns. The foliage chosen includes nine apricot-coloured peony leaves, three sprays of autumnal azalea leaves and five pieces of epimedium.

Begin with the flowers which will mark the length and choose those with curved stems so that the arrangement becomes linked to the container. Various

This arrangement is a table centre which has been adapted from the basic one and made more informal by placing bunches of flowers as if they were growing. The wicker trough has a plastic lining, and the wire netting is covered with bun moss, leaving some spaces where the flowers are placed. The tallest white daffodils are placed in first in two groups together with some of their leaves, then other flowers are put in at the ends to obtain the length, these being hyacinth and Christmas roses (*Helleborus niger*). Other bunches of flowers and foliage are added and placed diagonally across the basket. These include violets, heather and trails of ivy. The finished arrangement looks like a spring garden.

factors including the size of the table, the number of flowers available and the size of the trough will determine how far these stems should project over the edge of the container. The projection, however, should be the same either side. Two montbretias and one spray of hypericum should be placed on the left-hand side with one montbretia and two hypericum sprays on the right. The stems in each group should be of slightly varying length with a montbretia as the longest on the left and a hypericum as the longest on the right. The flowers in each group should be placed close together with the secondary stems of

both the montbretia and hypericum at each end of the container positioned diagonally opposite each other. All these stems should appear to radiate from the centre but they should only go halfway towards it so that they are secured through the netting but not necessarily into the florists' foam.

A small individual flower of a single chrysanthemum marks the widest point on one side of the width, with an individual flower from a double chrysanthemum spray on the other. These should not project over the edge as much as the flowers at either end of the length because the rectangular shape of the container needs to be taken into consideration. I have used an individual bud from a double chrysanthemum spray to establish the height. Its straight stem needs to be secured into the middle of the foam. As this arrangement is for a table centre, its height should not obscure the view of anyone across the table. Make a cluster of flowers around this chrysanthemum, keeping them close together and making each one a different length so

that the arrangement is quite pointed in the centre. Introduce, if possible, each kind of flower including one of each kind of dahlia.

Next return to the edge and connect up the main outline flowers with a broken line of flowers and berries. The flowers are grouped with the single chrysanthemums and montbretia together and the double chrysanthemums and hypericum together. Keep turning the arrangement all the time and ensure that the groupings go diagonally across the trough. The flower heads, when arranged, should gently curve round between the outline points maintaining a broken line. As the dahlias are the largest flowers they should be positioned near the centre of the arrangement. One kind is grouped with the montbretia and single chrysanthemums and the other with the hypericum and double chrysanthemums. Position two of each type with their groups near the centre on the outline edge on either side of the trough.

Cover the netting with some of the foliage and bring some out over the edge

These are the outline points of a table centre in a silver cake basket with a handle, which has a lining. The method of the arrangement is as for the basic table centre. The flowers are all pink, with a tulip the longest flower on one side and a carnation the longest on the opposite side. Hyacinth are kept nearer the centre.

of the container, then place in some of the berried subjects. The azalea, berberis and viburnum is grouped with the montbretia and single chrysanthemums and the Chinese lanterns and peony foliage with the double chrysanthemums and hypericum. Where there are only three pieces of a particular plant, place one on the edge on each side of the arrangement with the third quite near the centre. The lighter pieces of foliage and berries should be kept higher in the arrangement with the heavier pieces lower.

The remaining two dahlias of each type should be positioned so that there is one between the one on the edge and the centre one on either side and in either group. They should not be in a straight line but zig-zagged through the centre. Use the buds of the dahlias to lighten the arrangement.

Connect up the groups of flowers and merge them slightly through the centre. Check to see that the netting is completely covered and top up the trough to the rim with water.

L-shaped Arrangement

These arrangements can be quite narrow in depth and so they are useful for mantelpieces. They can also be positioned on the chancel steps in a church or on window-sills. Pairs can be arranged with the height on the right of one and on the left with the other. You may find it easier to do an L-shaped arrangement with the height on one particular side.

Troughs or low oval containers are the best for these arrangements. They will never look happy in vases with stems. My container is a black oval trough in heavy pottery. The summer flowers are blues and greens. There are nine stems of blue delphiniums, five blue irises, two bunches of blue cornflowers, twelve stems of *Alchemilla mollis* and some euphorbia. For the foliage I have chosen stripped lime and three lime-green hosta leaves. With this plant material I have a good variety of shape.

Fit your container with wire netting and place a pinholder in the left-hand corner for the taller stems. Begin three-

quarters of the way back and just in from the left-hand side. Secure a fairly straight piece of lime on to the pinholder. Ideally it should curve towards the left. Place a second shorter stem of lime to the left of the first and close into it. Establish the widest point on the right with a further stem of lime again securing it three-quarters of the way back in the container. This stem should curve naturally towards the surface on which the trough is standing and it should be roughly the same length as the tallest lime. A second shorter piece should be placed just in front of this one.

Next go back to the top of the arrangement and place a piece of alchemilla close to and shorter than the first lime and to the right-hand side of it. Then position another alchemilla low on the left-hand side. This will be the widest point here and it should project a little way over the edge of the trough. Place it in as horizontally as possible so that it connects trough and arrangement and secure it three-quarters of the way back making sure that it is in the water.

Flowers will be placed into the arrangement so that they graduate from the tallest stem to this widest one and so the stem length of this alchemilla must be long enough to accommodate them. A third alchemilla becomes the longest flower in the front in line with the tallest lime at the back. All the stems should radiate from the tallest stem though they should not touch it. If they did then you would not be able to position the centre flowers and leaves. They should go far enough into the trough to be able to drink sufficient water.

Start to place in the main flowers. Because the blue delphiniums are light in colour, pointed in shape and straight stemmed, place one of these so that it is taller than the tallest lime. A second shorter delphinium should go to the left of this flower with a cornflower to the right, a little shorter still. Place another delphinium close to the widest lime on the right-hand side, a little shorter than it. You will then have completed the basic outline which should not be exceeded.

The completed pink table centre. The flowers used are 15 tulips with grey *Senecio greyii* foliage, which are grouped one way, and seven carnations and five hyacinth with grey santolina foliage, which are grouped the opposite way. Make sure part of the handle can be seen.

47

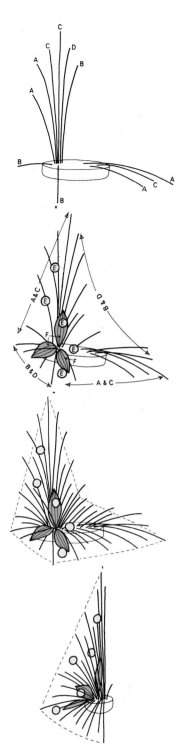

Finish this outline by placing the various groups around the edge with the smallest of each variety at the very edge, working the larger ones into the centre. From high on the left to low on the right go the lime, delphiniums and euphorbia. Retain the shape of the L by graduating these stems quickly from the tallest to the widest and bring the front ones well out around the edge. Arrange the alchemilla and cornflowers through the other way. A mixture of these two flowers should come around the front edge to meet up with the longest piece of alchemilla at the front. The flowers in the second group should be kept very short at the back edge to maintain the L shape. Make sure that there is a good variation of stem length in the outline so that you achieve a broken effect.

The blue irises are the centre flowers. These should tend to go in the same direction as the lime and delphiniums but should be kept nearer the centre. Place the first iris – one with a small flower and long stem – to the left side of the second delphinium. Then go to the opposite front edge and position a second small iris. These two flowers might still be in bud. A third iris should be placed in between these two in the centre of the container. The position of the fourth iris is between the centre and front ones but slightly to the right of both and shorter in the arrangement. The fifth iris should be placed between the tallest at the back and the centre one but slightly to the left of both of them and again shorter into the arrangement.

The three hosta leaves frame the irises. A small one should go under the iris at the front edge. Another small one goes at the back facing this one with the largest leaf a little to the side and low into the centre. Turn this leaf slightly sideways.

Then place some of the other foliage, together with the shorter alchemilla, to cover the netting. Connect up the groups through the centre and make sure that the flowers do not overshadow the outline. Some of the larger flowers can go very short into the arrangement but even with these try to get variation in stem length. The left of the arrangement, where the height is established, is the only place where the flowers can be built out as in a facing arrangement.

Above: A basic L-shaped arrangement, showing first the main outline points, secondly the placement of the centre flowers and leaves, and thirdly how the rest of the flowers and foliage are placed so as to keep the L shape. The fourth diagram shows the side view. The flowers and foliage used are lime (A), alchemilla (B), delphinium (C), cornflower (D), iris (E) and hosta (F).

48

Opposite page, right: The completed L-shaped arrangement in blues and lime green, in an oval black pottery trough.

Left and below: An L-shaped arrangement like this is suitable for a lidded basket because part of the lid can be seen. The outline points are achieved first. The flowers in this arrangement are all spray chrysanthemums, being the yellow and bronze single spray and larger bronze double spray varieties. Many of the flowers are used individually. The basket arrangement is constructed as for the basic L shape. The grouping consists of a single spray chrysanthemum and a variety of cotoneaster foliage going each way, with the double spray chrysanthemum and *Mahonia aquifolia* leaves near the centre.

Below: Line drawings to show a basic off-centre facing arrangement in a silver meat cover on a wrought-iron stand, in white and lime green flowers. The main outline points are shown first and then the flowers between the outline, with the centre flowers and leaves. Thirdly the overall shape is shown, and lastly a side view of how it should look. The flowers and foliage used are philadelphus (C), lime (D), roses (E), carnations (F), peonies (G) and hosta leaves (H).

Right: A picture of the completed off-centre facing arrangement in a silver meat cover.

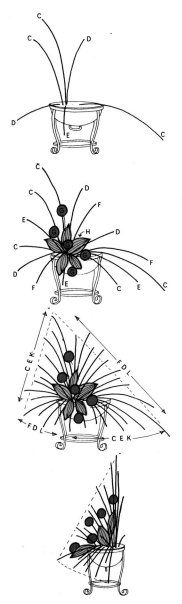

Face some of the flowers sideways to add interest. Do not overcrowd the plant material and distribute it equally. Make sure that the netting is covered at the back of the arrangement.

Off-centre Facing Arrangement

This arrangement could be described as a cross between the basic facing and the L shaped. It is asymmetrical. The tallest flower is not in the centre but about a quarter of the way in from either the right or left-hand edge of the container. A variety of containers could be used although baskets and boxes with lids should be avoided and the urn shape is perhaps too narrow at the top to show the flowers to their best advantage.

I have selected a silver meat cover which has had a wrought-iron stand made for it. Its broad oval shape makes it especially suitable for this type of arrangement. The flowers are white ones which look restful and cool in hot weather. The sprays of philadelphus have had some of the leaves removed from around the flowers to prevent wilting. Beware, however, of removing too many leaves as this would detract

from the attractiveness of the spray. Stripped lime is grouped in the opposite way to the philadelphus. Eleven roses make up the round flowers with the philadelphus and there are eleven carnations grouped with the lime. For the filler there is alchemilla with the philadelphus and roses and periwinkle (vinca) with the lime and carnations. Five white peonies are the main centre flowers with five large variegated hosta leaves.

A small piece of well-soaked florists' foam has been placed to the left-hand side of the container. I have chosen foam in preference to a pinholder as a screw from the handle has made the bottom of the meat cover uneven. The wire netting over the foam is secured to the wrought-iron stand in four places.

Begin with the outline flowers three-quarters of the way back in the container and a quarter of the way in from the left-hand side. Use a spray of philadelphus as the longest stem. This can curve slightly to the left. A second shorter piece of philadelphus can then be placed to the left of this, curving in line with the first. These two stems should be close together to obtain a pointed shape at the top. A stem of stripped lime is placed to the other side of the tallest philadelphus, again close to it and curving away from the centre. To define the width on the right side use a piece of philadelphus. This side is longer than the left and the stem should project well over the edge of the container with a downward curve. Also, because the meat cover is oval, the width of the finished arrangement should be slightly greater than the height. A piece of lime is used to mark the widest point on the left-hand side and this should be placed so that it too curves downwards. For the centre flower over the front edge of the container I have used a small-flowered rose, in line with the tallest flower at the back.

Fill in between these outline flowers by grouping the philadelphus and roses high on the left and low on the right with the lime and carnations arranged in the opposite direction. One side of the triangle will be longer than the other in this arrangement and the stem lengths should be decreased fairly quickly at the back to avoid a fan shape. Again a broken line should be aimed at with plenty of variation in stem length. The front should be rounded in shape but again one side will be longer than the other.

Use the peonies and hosta leaves to give weight and interest in the centre. The peonies should be positioned as follows: a small flower with a longish

A smaller off-centre facing arrangement in a dolphin vase with white spray carnations. The outline is established first. There are three kinds of foliage, ivy grouped one way, hebe the other, and peperomia leaves in the centre.

An adaptation of the basic off-centre facing arrangement in a pewter tankard. The shape is achieved first with the *Viburnum fragrans* and pink spray carnations, then the outline is filled in between by introducing the kaffir lilies with the *Viburnum fragrans*. The centre flowers are three pink gerbera and the centre leaves large pink-tinged ivy. The completed arrangement shows the grey foliage with the spray carnations and the hebe and santolina the opposite way, with flowers connecting through the centre. Make sure the handle of the tankard can be seen.

stem near the back against the first piece of philadelphus but shorter than it; another small flower over the front edge of the meat cover to the right of the first rose and nearly as long; a third peony between these two which becomes the centre flower; a larger shorter-stemmed flower between the front peony and the third and to the right of both; the last between the longest at the back and the centre one, to the left of them both.

The hosta leaves are positioned so that a small one comes over the front edge near the front peony. A second, larger leaf should be placed nearer the centre and turned sideways with a third – again small and longer stemmed – near the back peony so that it faces the front leaf. Another large one should be turned slightly and placed to one side of this with the fifth and largest leaf facing sideways in the centre.

Use some of the foliage in their correct groups to cover the netting. Some of the rose leaves could be used with the roses. Connect the two groups through the centre and again have plenty of variation of stem length, with the flowers evenly spaced and not too close together. Turn some of the flowers sideways to add interest and keep the larger ones lower in the arrangement. Check to see that all the netting is covered.

Facing Arrangement in an Urn

Although this arrangement is similar to the facing arrangement in a tazza which I have already described, I have included it in my eight basic arrangements because the shape of the urn demands that the proportions are different. The urn is in grey pottery and because this container is comparatively tall and thin, it only needs wire netting in which to secure the flowers. Neither a pinholder nor florists' foam are necessary.

I have chosen flowers in clashing reds – blue-reds and yellow-reds. There are fifteen stems of kaffir lilies which are pointed in shape and blue-red. The other pointed flower is orange montbretia. There are also two stems of red spray chrysanthemums, five dark red dahlias, three pieces of mountain spinach, three pieces of pyracantha with orange-red berries, five stems of wild rose hips, three pieces of bryony, three pieces of honeysuckle berries and three stems of skimmia berries. The foliage is in autumnal shades – seven stems of prunus and five pieces of *Ajuga repens atropurpurea*. There are also three bergenia leaves for the centre.

Begin this arrangement by placing a stem of montbretia, which measures between one-and-a-half times and twice

Below and right: An arrangement in an urn with clashing red flowers. The flowers and foliage used are montbretia (A), kaffir lilies (B), dahlias (C), bergenia (D), chrysanthemum (E), pyracantha (F), bryony (G), skimmia (H), prunus (J), hips (K), mountain spinach (L), honeysuckle (M) and ajuga (N).

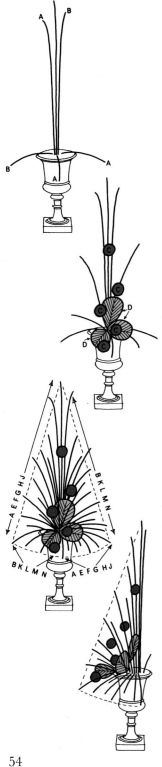

the height of the urn, three-quarters of the way back in the centre of the container. Place a shorter-stemmed kaffir lily to the right of this and another montbretia to the left. These three flowers should be close together to secure them through the same hole in the netting.

Next the width of the arrangement should be established by placing a curved-stem montbretia low down on the right-hand side, three-quarters of the way back in the container. The stem of this flower should be fairly short so that the finished arrangement echoes the

54

elegant shape of the urn. The overall width of an arrangement in an urn should be a little over half the height. On the opposite side place a kaffir lily which is the same length as the montbretia on the right-hand side. Another montbretia should be brought well out over the front of the container in line with the tallest flower at the back. The main outline flowers will now be in position and, as with all arrangements, all the subsequent stems should appear to radiate from the tallest at the back. This is a little more difficult with a narrow-necked vase.

Introduce the berries into the arrangement and secure all the material used to fill in the back outline three-quarters of the way back in the container. Graduate the length of the stems down quite quickly at the back edge to avoid a rounded top. Create a good semi-circle around the front edge extending from the widest-placed flowers to the longest at the front. I have grouped the montbretia and chrysanthemums with the berries of pyracantha, bryony and skimmia and the foliage of prunus high on the left and low on the right and the kaffir lilies, hips, mountain spinach, honeysuckle berries and ajuga high on the right and low on the left.

Place some of each kind of flower and berry in the outline but keep particularly curved stems like those of the bryony at the front edge of the arrangement and lower down. The straighter-stemmed hips will look well at the back and any curved stems of hips can be used to fill in the outline on the left-hand front edge.

When you have achieved a satisfactory outline put in the main flowers. A fairly small dahlia should be placed high but centred in the arrangement with another small flower to the left of the centre flower at the front. Zig-zag the other dahlias to meet up with these two flowers but keep them close through the centre. The three bergenia leaves are used to frame the dahlias. One should go over the edge at the front left; another, the largest, turned sideways in the centre; and the third should be placed at the back of the arrangement facing the one at the front.

At this stage fill up with foliage to cover the netting, keeping the prunus high on the left and low on the right, and

the ajuga the opposite way. Connect up the groups of flowers and berries remembering to turn some of the plant material sideways to keep the arrangement looking more natural. When there are only three pieces of a particular flower to be used, as there are in several

A modern arrangement in a bamboo cylinder with three spider or Singapore orchids and three bergenia leaves. Keep the shape narrow as for a basic urn arrangement.

cases in this arrangement, have one high at the back of the arrangement, one low over the opposite side and one in the centre. Try to get good variation of stem length with the long stems bearing the smaller flowers and the shorter stems the larger ones. Do not make the main flowers in the centre look too obvious but merge the groups through them. If the centre flowers stand out too much the eye will rest on them and this will spoil the effect of the composition.

Finish by checking that the netting is covered.

Facing Arrangement in a Basket with a Handle

When creating an arrangement in a basket with a handle every care must be taken to ensure that the handle, or at least part of it, is seen when the arrangement is completed.

A variation of the facing arrangement in an urn. In this green urn five gladioli have been kept near the centre of the container but gradually made shorter as they come forward, in the second picture 'sweeping' through with the *Hamamelis mollis* from high on the left to low on the right front edge. This gives a more interesting line than making it symmetrical.

My basket has a baking-tin lining and this has been fitted with wire netting and a fairly large pinholder placed three-quarters of the way back in the centre to hold the heavier and longer stems.

I have chosen spring flowers because their yellow colouring and informality complement the colour and nature of the basket. To give added interest with the daffodils, narcissi and tulips, I am using some branches of hazel catkins and forsythia. These lend their pointed shapes to be grouped with the rounded flowers of the daffodils and tulips. The arrangement requires one-and-a-half bunches of large yellow daffodils, one-and-a-half bunches of the orange-centred narcissus Fortune and one bunch of the narcissus Soleil d'Or. This last variety is distinctive with several small flowers to each stem and provides a different shape. The five yellow tulips are treated as the main

To complete the arrangement in the urn some bergenia leaves have been placed in the centre and some *Hamamelis mollis* arranged through the centre. High on the right to low on the left has been placed some brown tinged azalea foliage to pick up the colour of the brown centre of the *Hamamelis*.

57

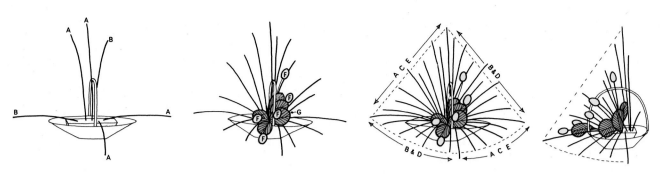

Line drawings to show a facing arrangement in a basket with a handle. The first diagram shows the six outline points, the second the flowers added on the outline and the centre flowers and leaves. The third shows the overall shape and the fourth a side view of how the arrangement should look. The flowers and foliage used are forsythia (A), catkins (B), Fortune narcissi (C), daffodils (D), Soleil d'Or narcissi (E), tulips (F) and bergenia leaves (G).

centre flowers and the foliage is tree ivy, trailing ivy and five bergenia leaves.

The main outline points are established with the hazel and forsythia. The height is determined by a piece of forsythia which should be placed so that it comes above the handle, to the left side of it and close in to it, three-quarters of the way back in the basket. It may be necessary to make the branches of forsythia and hazel less heavy at the top by pruning some of the sprigs away. This will help to keep the arrangement lighter at the top and a better shape. Pieces cut away from a branch can be used later in the arrangement in helping to cover the wire netting. Place a second, shorter piece of forsythia next to the first, again on the left side of the handle. A twig of catkins is placed on the opposite side to the first forsythia and to the right of the handle. This should be shorter than the second forsythia. If these stems have a natural curve use them so that they turn away from the centre of the basket. Never allow the branches to curve into the centre as they will then cross the stems of the centre flowers and will not appear to radiate from the tallest branch.

Determine the width of the arrangement by placing a piece of forsythia on the right and a twig of hazel catkins on the left. The length of these stems should be such that the overall width is slightly more than the height so that the shape of the finished arrangement is fairly low and flowing to echo the line of the container. Secure both these stems three-quarters of the way back in the container so that they come horizontally out over the edge of the basket. Place a piece of forsythia, which has been lightened by pruning, well over the front edge of the container so that it is on the opposite side of the handle to the tallest forsythia at the back. If this front piece is placed on the same side of the handle as the tallest branch, the arrangement would appear

shorter on one side than the other and therefore unbalanced.

When you have established the main outline points, place more pieces of both forsythia and catkins around the edge to achieve a triangular rather than a fan shape. All the stems should radiate from the back but they should not touch the back stems as you will then have difficulty in positioning the flowers without moving the established points. Each stem should be placed so that its head is in the exact position where it is required. Do not place a stem and then attempt to move its head into a slightly different position.

The forsythia is positioned on the left side at the back of the basket and on the right side at the front, with the catkins placed in the opposite direction. Do not put in any pieces which are longer than the main outline or overshadowing it and aim for a semi-circular shape around the front of the basket.

Once the outline of twigs is in place, you can start to position the flowers. A comparatively small flower is needed as the longest one and I have chosen a small flower of Fortune. The second flower is a shorter-stemmed Fortune placed to one side of the first and both these flowers are positioned to the left of the handle. The third flower at the top is the smallest of the daffodils and this is placed to the right of the handle. A good guide to the length is to make each of these stems half a head shorter than the one before. The flowers marking the width are positioned next with a small Fortune, cut a little shorter than the forsythia, marking the widest flower point on the right, and a small daffodil, a little shorter than the catkins, determining the widest point on the left. Another small Fortune should be placed with the longest piece of forsythia in the front, on the same side of the handle. Again it should be cut a little shorter than the forsythia.

The completed basket of mixed spring flowers with foliage of tree and trailing ivy. Part of the handle should be seen.

Next put in some flowers on the outline taking care to keep the shape established by the forsythia and catkins. The Soleil d'Or should be grouped in the same direction as the Fortune with the daffodils going the opposite way. When the outline is completed position the tulips. One should go at the back of the arrangement on the same side of the handle as the daffodils. Another goes over the front edge on the opposite side of the handle. The third is placed in the centre just above the handle so that it breaks the line of the handle slightly and makes a straight line with the first two tulips. The fourth tulip comes under the handle between the front tulip and the third tulip and the fifth is between the longest tulip at the back and the third. Do not place the fourth and fifth tulips in a straight line with the first three.

The five bergenia leaves are arranged near the centre with the tulips. The first, a small-sized one, should come over the front edge of the basket to the left of the handle. The second, a little larger, is placed further into the basket to the left side of the first and turned slightly to face the side. The largest, turned sideways, goes into the centre of the arrangement to the right with the fourth leaf at the back to the right of the handle and facing towards the first leaf. The last leaf should go a little further forward than the fourth, to the right and turned slightly sideways.

Next group some of the trailing ivy through the arrangement with the daffodils so that it comes well out over the edge of the basket and is high at the back. Use some shorter pieces through the centre. The tree ivy should go the opposite way with the Fortune and Soleil d'Or.

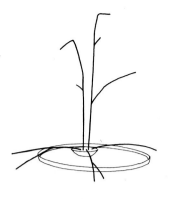 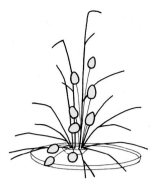 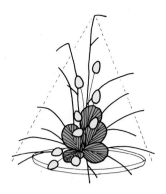 

Connect up the groupings so that they merge in the centre. Put some stems of forsythia and catkins through the arrangement and place some of the little pieces which have been trimmed away from the main stems lower down. The daffodil and narcissi leaves can be grouped in threes with differing lengths and five such bunches of threes would be sufficient. The tulip leaves can also be used. It is possible to open one of the tulip flowers by turning back the petals and this creates the effect of a larger flower to give weight in the centre of the arrangement. Do not do this to any more, however, as it can look artificial. In order to keep the handle free, this arrangement is not built out to the same extent as the basic facing.

Finish, as usual, by checking that the netting is covered, especially at the back, and top up the tin with water.

Line Arrangement

Line arrangements should not be confused with Japanese flower arrangements. They are secured on to a pinholder which sits on a flat dish and are much simpler than the massed arrangements previously described. They generally contain only one type of flower and are very attractive in a modern home setting, although with care they can look equally well against traditional furniture.

This type of arrangement can be created with flowers alone but I especially like to add twigs. The branches for the arrangement shown here are those of the alder, cut before the catkin buds opened. There are also nine orange Apeldoorn tulips and five bergenia leaves which have a slight orange tinge to them.

I have used a round woven tray for the base and on this has been placed, slightly to the left of centre, a small metal container to hold a large pinholder. Empty, painted salmon tins are particularly useful in this context if you have nothing else available. I have five pinky-orange pebbles to hide the metal container.

The outline is established with the alder. Choose a reasonably straight piece as the first and longest stem although a slight curve away from the centre at the top is an advantage. Secure this three-quarters of the way back on the pinholder in the centre. If this branch has another attached to it this may be considered as the second or third stem at the back of the arrangement depending on the length of this attached twig. Should it be necessary to trim away any side twigs, do this as close to the main branch as possible and try to have these cuts at the back of the branch when it is arranged. The light wood of a cut can look very ugly against the darker bark.

Next either position the second or third branch close to the first or both if the first branch had no convenient side twigs. The natural curve of these branches should be away from the centre.

The width is established by placing a piece of alder low to the left so that it comes over the edge of the tray and is close to it, thus ensuring that the arrangement and tray become one unit visually. Position another stem of alder on the right-hand side but make sure that it does not project so far over the edge as that on the left. It is better if the finished arrangement does not look too symmetrical and it is for this reason that the water-holding container was put to the left of centre on the tray. The overall

61

width should be slightly less than the height. A piece of alder should also be positioned in the front, in line with the tallest at the back.

Fill in this main outline with alder at the back to achieve a triangular rather than a fan shape, i.e. decrease the lengths of the stems quite quickly. Also connect the widest point to the centre taking care not to outstep the main outline. Vary the stem lengths to achieve a broken line and do not overcrowd them as it is important that the tray should be seen in the finished arrangement.

Now add the tulips. Take one with a small flower and a long stem. This may be difficult to find as inevitably it is the larger flowers which have the longer stems. However, it is essential to have a small flower as the longest at the back of the arrangement or it could easily look top heavy. Place this stem close to the longest alder; if possible, it should curve in the same direction as this branch. A second tulip with a larger flower but shorter stem should then be positioned to one side of the first tulip, the same side as the second piece of alder. A third flower, larger and shorter stemmed still, goes to the other side. Each of these flowers is secured progressively a little further forward on the pinholder.

This is a piece of driftwood, which makes an excellent container for an arrangement of flowers. A small tin with a pinholder in it is placed on the wood and held in position with Bostik Blu-tack.

Next choose a small flower and secure this low at the front to the left of the front stem of alder with the flower touching the edge of the tray. Place the stem sideways on to the pinholder. A second tulip with a larger flower and shorter stem should be positioned to the right of this front flower with a third, larger and shorter stemmed still, to the left of the front flower. These last two flowers are slightly higher than the first.

Then, in the centre, place three tulips to join the back and front groups together. A small-flowered, reasonably long-stemmed flower should be positioned in line with the flowers at the centre back

and front. A larger, shorter-stemmed flower goes to the right of this one, further back on the pinholder with an even larger but shorter-stemmed flower to the left of centre and towards the front. When completed the tulip flowers should be equidistant. It is especially important in this type of arrangement to position the flowers exactly right as there are so few of them.

The five bergenia leaves are needed to give added weight in the centre and to frame the flowers, and these are positioned next. Place a small but long-stemmed leaf at the back near to the first tulip and reaching to about half way up

The flowers arranged in the container on the driftwood are purple statice and mauvey iris with zebrina foliage. They are positioned as for an L-shaped arrangement, taking care the shape of the driftwood is seen when the arrangement is finished.

63

An idea for a line arrangement which includes grapes. There are three sanseviera leaves with three orange lilies in the centre and five bergenia leaves. Anchor the bunch of grapes by twisting wire round the stem and putting it in the pin-holder, which is in a small container on the green plate.

its stem. Position another small leaf with a longish stem against the first flower at the front edge so that it is shorter than the tulip. A third leaf goes to the right of the first and shorter than it with a fourth of similar size to the left of the second. The fifth, largest leaf should be cut very short and placed sideways into the centre of the arrangement.

Put the finishing touches by placing more alder branches attractively between the tulips and if any of the pin-holder or the container can be seen use some tulip leaves to cover them. Fill in the back of the arrangement with leaves, and finally arrange the pebbles from the edge of the tray towards the container so the eye is drawn towards the centre.